THE

Little

BOOK

OF

Chocolate

summersdale

THE LITTLE BOOK OF CHOCOLATE

Text by Hannah Adams

An Hachette UK Company
www.hachette.co.uk

Summersdale Publishers Ltd
Part of Octopus Publishing Group Limited
Carmelite House
50 Victoria Embankment
LONDON
EC4Y 0DZ
UK

www.summersdale.com

Printed and bound in China

ISBN: 978-1-78783-576-4

Substantial discounts on bulk quantities of Summersdale books are available to corporations, professional associations and other organizations. For details contact general enquiries: telephone: +44 (0) 1243 771107 or email: enquiries@summersdale.com.

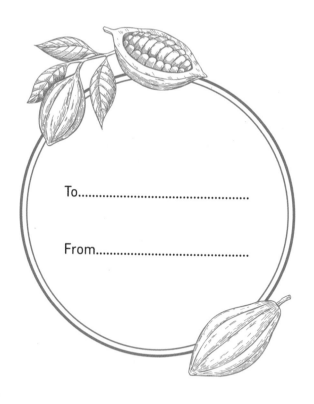

To...

From.....................................

CHOCOLATE: FOOD OF THE GODS

Chocolate is made from the fermented, dried and roasted seeds of the cacao tree. The tree, *Theobroma cacao* (which translates as "food of the gods"), can grow to between 4 and 8 metres (13–26 feet) high. The cacao pods that grow from the tree have rough leathery rinds, sweet inner pulp and around 30–50 light or dark purple seeds. These seeds must be dried and fully fermented before cocoa solids and cocoa butter can be extracted to form chocolate.

The cacao tree grows in tropical climates with regular rainfall. For this reason, most of the world's cocoa is grown close to the equator, with the main producers being the Ivory Coast, Ghana, Ecuador, Cameroon, Nigeria and Indonesia.

CACAO vs COCOA

These terms are often used interchangeably, but there is an important difference between them. To put it simply, cacao refers to the seed of the *Theobroma cacao* tree and is the name for the unprocessed beans. These can be eaten raw, but they're very bitter. Cocoa is the name for the processed beans of the cacao tree and the main ingredient in chocolate.

A BRIEF HISTORY OF CHOCOLATE

The humble seed of the cacao tree has a rich and diverse history, though no one is quite sure where and when it began.

Generally, it is thought that the cacao tree was first domesticated over 4,000 years ago by the Mokaya and the Olmec civilizations in Mesoamerica. By the eighth century AD, the Mayan civilization had made chocolate an integral part of their culture and society (even using it in sacred rituals of birth, marriage and death). The preferred way to consume the cacao seeds was by roasting and grinding them, and mixing them with chillies, water and cornmeal. The Mayans called this thick, foamy drink *xocolatl* ("bitter water"), from which our word "chocolate" is thought to derive.

By the fifteenth century, the Aztecs had taken over a large part of Mesoamerica. The Aztecs started to use cacao beans as currency. However, it wasn't until the sixteenth century, when Spain began to colonize the Americas, that Europeans encountered this sacred tree. Following the Spanish conquest, chocolate began to be imported to Europe, where the bean was rumoured to have nutritious, medicinal and aphrodisiac properties. Too bitter for some, the Spaniards tried sweetening the ground seeds with honey or sugar, and many found the flavour to be far more palatable.

With a growing demand for chocolate across Europe, a booming slave market for its manufacture developed. Over the next few centuries, cocoa plantations spread across the equatorial regions of South America, and processes were developed to speed up production.

Once machines had vastly improved the manufacturing process, chocolate began to be consumed as a food, more than as a drink, and new flavours and textures were developed.

In 2019, it was estimated that the global spend on chocolate was approximately £104.6 billion ($140 billion) and the figure is continually rising!

FROM SEED TO BAR: HOW CHOCOLATE IS MADE

Chocolate is made from the seeds of the cacao tree, but most of us enjoy it in a very different form. Here's how it goes from humble bean to delicious bar, in six simple steps.

FERMENTATION: once picked, cocoa pods are split open to scoop out the beans and fleshy white pulp inside. The beans and pulp are left to ferment outside for a week to ensure the beans are prevented from germinating, and to allow them to develop their "chocolatey" flavour.

DRYING: the beans are sun-dried (this usually takes around seven days) until they are ready to be shipped from the plantation to the factory.

ROASTING: to develop the flavour of the beans further, they are roasted. This is the stage at which a chocolate manufacturer can most directly affect the flavour of the final chocolate.

WINNOWING: the cacao nib is removed from its shell (which puffs up during the roasting process and makes it easier to remove).

GRINDING: the nibs are ground into a liquid called "cocoa liquor". The "liquor" must be passed through a filter to purify it, at which point it starts to look a little like melted chocolate, but tastes very bitter. The chocolate is ground further to prevent it from being too grainy. At this point, a chocolate manufacturer would add different ingredients to the mix, such as milk powder, sugar or other flavourings.

TEMPERING: this ensures the chocolate solidifies properly and is a very technical process. Broadly, tempering chocolate involves heating it to melting point, crystallizing a part of it, adding the seed crystals back in to the chocolate and letting it set.

BUYING ETHICALLY AND SUSTAINABLY

Historically, chocolate production has involved some unsavoury truths. As with many other consumer products, chocolate manufacturers have come under scrutiny in recent years for not providing their employees with safe working conditions and a fair wage. Fortunately, movements such as Fairtrade have helped to make cocoa farming more sustainable by guaranteeing minimum prices to farmers and investing in local communities. Fairtrade labelling also helps consumers to make responsible choices when purchasing chocolate.

Beyond the human focus in chocolate production, the cocoa sector faces a few other challenges, including poor soil-fertility management, improper use of chemicals, and deforestation. To combat this, organizations such as UTZ Certified work with major chocolate producers to try to create efficient sustainability programmes and effective traceability in cocoa production. In fact, UTZ Certified is now the largest programme in the world for sustainable cocoa, and many global chocolate manufacturers have started to embrace sustainability and ethical farming.

So, the good news is that we can still go on enjoying our favourite treat, but we should all do our absolute best to avoid supporting companies whose practices are not ethical or sustainable. The power is in our hands as consumers to choose to buy chocolate from manufacturers who are transparent about their production processes.

STORING CHOCOLATE

Assuming you can resist eating the chocolate in your possession for more than 24 hours, it's important to know how to keep your chocolate as fresh as possible. Follow these tips for effective chocolate storage:

STORE IN A COOL, DRY PLACE
As long as chocolate is kept at a consistent temperature (ideally between 15–20°C/59–68°F), the emulsion of cocoa solids and cocoa butter can remain stable for a few months.

KEEP IT IN AN AIRTIGHT CONTAINER
Oxygen will oxidize chocolate, which can cause unpleasant flavours to develop.

DON'T KEEP IT IN THE FRIDGE
Not only does chocolate absorb odours easily, but the moisture can also lead to discolouration (when the sugar rises to the surface) – this is called "blooming". If you must refrigerate it in order

to stop it melting, wrap it in cling film or a beeswax wrap and put it in an airtight container.

USE THE FREEZER IF YOU MUST

To extend the life of chocolate for an additional six months to a year beyond its use-by date, it is possible to freeze it. Refrigerate the chocolate using the steps above for at least 24 hours and then transfer it to the freezer. Reverse the process to defrost the chocolate.

IF STORED PROPERLY, HOW LONG DOES CHOCOLATE LAST?

Dark chocolate: up to two years

Milk and white chocolate: up to one year

Chocolate chips: up to two years

Home-made chocolates: up to six months (as long as they don't include dairy ingredients)

Cocoa powder: up to three years

CONVERSIONS AND MEASUREMENTS

All the conversions in the tables below are close approximations. When folliwing a recipe, always stick to one unit of measurement, and do not alternate between them.

IMPERIAL–METRIC CONVERSIONS: WEIGHTS

½ oz	10 g
¾ oz	20 g
1 oz	25 g
2 oz	50 g
3 oz	75 g
1 lb	450 g
1 lb 8 oz	700 g
2 lb	900 g
3 lb	1.35 kg

IMPERIAL–METRIC CONVERSIONS: VOLUME

Teaspoon (tsp, t)	5 ml
Tablespoon (tbsp, T)	15 ml
2 fl. oz	75 ml
5 fl. oz (¼ pint)	150 ml
10 fl. oz (½ pint)	275 ml
1 pint	570 ml
1¼ pints	725 ml
1¾ pints	1 litre
2 pints	1.2 litres

IMPERIAL–METRIC CONVERSIONS: **LENGTH**

1 inch	2.5 cm
3 inches	7.6 cm
5 inches	12.7 cm
7 inches	17.8 cm
9 inches	22.9 cm
11 inches	27.9 cm
13 inches	33.02 cm

TEMPERATURES

Gas Mark	Celsius	Fahrenheit
1	140	275
2	150	300
3	170	325
4	180	350
5	190	375
6	200	400
7	220	425
8	230	450
9	245	475
10	260	500

Simple Chocolate Mousse

SERVES 4

INGREDIENTS

- 150 g 70% dark chocolate, plus extra to serve
- 6 egg whites
- 2 tbsp golden caster sugar
- 4 tbsp crème fraîche, to serve
- Mint leaves (optional)

METHOD

- Break the chocolate into a heatproof bowl on top of a pan of simmering water (make sure the bowl isn't touching the water), stirring occasionally until melted. Once fully melted, remove from the heat.

- Whisk the egg whites, add in the sugar and whisk again until the mixture forms stiff peaks.

- Add a heaped tablespoon of the egg whites to the melted chocolate and mix well with a spatula, working quickly so that the chocolate doesn't harden.

- Continue to carefully fold in the egg whites one tablespoon at a time.

- Spoon into four glasses and set in the fridge for 2–3 hours.

- Serve with a spoonful of crème fraîche, dark chocolate shavings and a mint leaf (optional).

I just love chocolate. It's God's apology for broccoli.

RICHARD PAUL EVANS

CHOCOLATEY FACT

It takes around 400 cacao beans to make
454 grams (1 pound) of chocolate.

Gluten-Free Chocolate Cupcakes

MAKES 12

INGREDIENTS

For the cake:

- 250 g unsalted butter
- 250 g caster sugar
- 4 eggs
- 250 g gluten-free self-raising flour
- 2 tsp vanilla extract
- 3 tbsp cocoa powder

For the buttercream:

- 100 g milk chocolate
- 200 g unsalted butter
- 400 g icing sugar
- 4 tbsp cocoa powder
- 1 tbsp milk

METHOD

- Heat the oven to 190°C and line a cupcake tin with cupcake cases.

- Place the butter and sugar into a large mixing bowl and beat until creamy.

- Beat in the eggs and then fold the flour into the mixture.

- Add the vanilla and cocoa powder and mix well.

- Divide the mixture evenly between the cupcake cases.

- Bake in the preheated oven for 20 minutes, until the cakes have risen and a skewer comes out clean.

- While the cupcakes are baking, make the buttercream by breaking the chocolate into a heatproof bowl and placing it over a pan of simmering water (make sure the bowl isn't touching the water).

- Stir the chocolate constantly and, when melted, leave it to cool for 5 minutes.

- In another bowl, beat together the butter and icing sugar until creamy.

- Sift the cocoa powder into the mixture, then stir in the melted chocolate and the milk, mixing until smooth.

- Leave the cupcakes to cool completely before placing the buttercream into a piping bag and icing the cupcakes.

- Serve immediately, or store in an airtight container at room temperature for up to two days.

Chocolate

MAKES
EVERYTHING
BETTER

· · · · · · · · · · ·

Chemically speaking,
chocolate really is the
world's perfect food.

MICHAEL LEVINE

Easy Chocolate Truffles

VEGAN

MAKES 20

INGREDIENTS
- 300 g dark chocolate chips
- 240 ml coconut cream
- 50 g cocoa powder, to coat

METHOD
- Place the chocolate chips into a mixing bowl.

- Heat the coconut cream to a simmer (either on the hob or in the microwave).

- Pour the simmering cream over the chocolate chips and leave for a minute to melt before stirring the mix to make a chocolate sauce.

- Place the mixture in the fridge to set for 3–4 hours (it needs to be solid).

- When set, use a spoon to scoop out even amounts of the ganache and roll them into balls with your hands.

- Roll the balls in cocoa powder until covered.

- Return to the fridge to set again (1–2 hours) and serve.

- These truffles will last for up to six days if stored in an airtight container in the fridge.

CARAMELS ARE ONLY
A FAD. CHOCOLATE IS
A PERMANENT THING.

MILTON S. HERSHEY

CHOCOLATEY FACT

The Ivory Coast and Ghana produce over
60 per cent of global cocoa supply.

White Chocolate and Berry Cheesecake

SERVES 8

INGREDIENTS

For the base:

- 70 g unsalted butter, melted, plus extra for greasing
- 150 g digestive biscuits

For the filling:

- 250 g cream cheese (mascarpone, if possible)
- 300 ml double cream
- 2 tsp vanilla extract
- 225 g white chocolate
- 200 g mixed berries, to serve

METHOD

- Grease a 20-cm springform cake tin with butter, then line with baking paper.

- For the base, place the biscuits in a sandwich bag and use a rolling pin to crush them until they resemble breadcrumbs, then put them and the melted butter into a mixing bowl and stir.

- Spoon the biscuit mixture onto the base of the lined cake tin and press with the back of a spoon until level. Cover and chill in the fridge while making the cheesecake filling.

- Put the cream cheese and double cream into a mixing bowl and whisk the mixture until it forms soft peaks. Mix in the vanilla.

- Break the chocolate into a heatproof bowl and set it over a pan of simmering water (make sure the bowl isn't touching the water). Stir until just melted, then set aside for 5–7 minutes.

- Pour the chocolate on top of the cream cheese mixture and stir until well combined.

- Spoon the filling onto the biscuit base and smooth the top. Cover with cling film and chill for at least 8 hours (preferably overnight).

- To serve, carefully remove from the tin and arrange the berries on the top of the cheesecake.

My birthstone

IS A CACAO
BEAN

. . . .

There are four basic food groups: milk chocolate, dark chocolate, white chocolate and chocolate truffles.

ANONYMOUS

Dark Chocolate Fondue

VEGAN

SERVES 6

INGREDIENTS
- 225 g dark chocolate
- 300 ml non-dairy milk
- Pinch of salt
- 1 tsp vanilla extract

METHOD
- Break up the chocolate into small pieces and place in a heatproof mixing bowl.

- Heat the milk in a saucepan over a low heat, until warm. Add the salt.

- Remove the milk from the heat and pour over the chocolate, ensuring that all pieces are fully covered.

- Cover the bowl and set aside for 3–5 minutes.

- Add the vanilla extract to the chocolate mixture and whisk to combine.

- Serve immediately with your choice of foods to dip – fruit like strawberries or banana work well, as do cake pieces and marshmallows.

STRENGTH IS
THE CAPACITY
TO BREAK A
CHOCOLATE
BAR INTO FOUR
PIECES... AND THEN
EAT JUST ONE.

JUDITH VIORST

CHOCOLATEY FACT

Over 3.5 million tonnes of cocoa is
produced annually across the world.

Chocolate Soufflé

MAKES 4

INGREDIENTS

- Unsalted butter, for greasing
- 65 g granulated sugar, plus extra for lining
- 175 g dark chocolate (minimum 70% cocoa solids)
- 4 egg yolks
- 8 egg whites
- Icing sugar, for dusting

METHOD

- Heat the oven to 190°C and set your oven rack in the lowest position in your oven.

- Butter four ramekins and coat with a little granulated sugar (this will help prevent the soufflé from sticking to the dish).

- Break the chocolate into a heatproof bowl and set it over a pan of simmering water (make sure the bowl isn't touching the water). Stir continuously until the chocolate has melted.

- Remove the chocolate from the heat and let it cool down slightly.

- Once cooled a little, whisk the egg yolks into the chocolate.

- Using an electric whisk, beat the egg whites in a separate bowl until they form soft peaks. Then, add the sugar one tablespoon at a time and beat until the peaks are stiff and glossy.

- Gradually fold the egg whites into the chocolate mixture until just incorporated.

- Pour the mixture into the prepared ramekins and bake for around 30 minutes (or until puffed up and just cracking on the surface).

- Dust with icing sugar and serve immediately.

I WOULD GIVE UP
CHOCOLATE, BUT I'M
NOT A QUITTER

Anything is good if it's made of chocolate.

JO BRAND

Chocolate Macarons

MAKES 12

INGREDIENTS

For the shells:
- 125 g icing sugar
- 1 tbsp cocoa powder
- 100 g ground almonds
- 2 egg whites

For the filling:
- 50 g dark chocolate
- 2 tbsp skimmed milk, warmed slightly

METHOD

- Pre-heat the oven to 160°C and line a large baking tray with baking paper.

- Sift the icing sugar and cocoa powder into a bowl and stir in the ground almonds.

- In a separate bowl, whisk the egg whites until they form stiff peaks, then fold in the dry ingredients.

- Fill an icing bag with the mixture and pipe 24 discs (around 3 cm wide) on to the baking sheet, leaving some room between each one as they will expand in the oven.

- Leave the mixture to dry for 20 minutes, then bake for 15 minutes, or until the macarons feel firm to the touch and peel off the paper easily.

- For the filling, break the chocolate into a heatproof bowl and set it over a pan of simmering water (make sure the bowl isn't touching the water). Stir in the warm milk until the mixture is smooth and leave it to cool so that it thickens a little.

- Use the filling to sandwich the macarons together, and store in an airtight container in the fridge for up to three days. Freeze the macarons for up to six months.

DESSERTS ARE THE MOST CRUCIAL PART OF ANY MEAL.

LINDA SUNSHINE

CHOCOLATEY FACT

Cacao has over 600 flavour compounds.
Red wine, by comparison, has only 200.

Chocolate and Raspberry Flapjacks

MAKES 12

INGREDIENTS

- 200 g unsalted butter, plus extra for greasing
- 300 g golden syrup
- 450 g rolled oats
- 100 g freeze-dried raspberries
- 100 g dark chocolate chips

METHOD

- Preheat the oven to 180°C. Grease a square baking tin (23 x 23 cm) with butter and line the base and sides with baking paper.

- Place the butter and syrup in a saucepan and heat until the mixture starts to boil, stirring continuously. Remove the mixture from the heat and pour into a mixing bowl.

- Add in the oats, then the freeze-dried raspberries, mixing until well combined.

- Scrape the mixture into the prepared baking tin and make sure the surface is even.

- Bake for 45 minutes, or until golden-brown, then leave to cool slightly.

- Run a knife around the edges of the tin and cut the flapjack into 12 squares. Set aside again to cool completely.

- While the flapjacks are cooling, place the chocolate chips in a heatproof bowl over a pan of simmering water (make sure the bowl isn't touching the water), and stir until the chocolate has melted.

- Turn the flapjacks out onto a wire rack and drizzle over the melted chocolate.

- Allow the chocolate to set and store in an airtight container for up to three days.

But first,

CHOCOLATE

. . . .

CHOCOLATE IS THE ONLY AROMATHERAPY I NEED.

JASMINE HEILER

Chocolate Chip Cookies

MAKES 30

INGREDIENTS

- 150 g unsalted butter, softened
- 80 g light muscovado sugar
- 80 g granulated sugar
- 1 tsp vanilla extract
- 1 egg
- 230 g plain flour
- ½ tsp bicarbonate of soda
- 250 g dark chocolate chips

METHOD

- Heat the oven to 190°C and line two trays with baking paper.

- Put the butter into a bowl with the sugar and beat until creamy.

- Add in the vanilla extract and egg.

- Sift in the flour and the bicarbonate of soda and fold the mixture with a spoon.

- Add the chocolate chips and mix well.

- Scoop the dough a tablespoon at a time onto your pre-lined trays. Leave some room between each cookie as they will expand in the oven.

- Bake for 8–10 minutes until the edges are light brown but the centre is still soft.

- Serve immediately, or store in an airtight container at room temperature for up to three days.

SEIZE THE
MOMENT.
REMEMBER ALL
THOSE WOMEN ON
THE *TITANIC* WHO
WAVED OFF THE
DESSERT CART.

ERMA BOMBECK

CHOCOLATEY FACT

The inventor of the chocolate chip cookie, Ruth Wakefield, sold her recipe to Nestlé for one dollar and a lifetime supply of chocolate.

Sweet Potato Brownies

VEGAN

MAKES 16

INGREDIENTS

- 250 g sweet potato
- 125 g almond butter
- 125 g cocoa powder
- 200 g caster sugar
- 50 g plain flour
- 1 tsp baking powder
- 1 tsp vanilla extract
- 75 g dark chocolate chips

METHOD

- Peel and cut the sweet potatoes into 5 cm pieces, then place them in a large saucepan with just enough water to cover them.

- Bring the potatoes to the boil for 15 minutes, or until you can easily stick a knife through them.

- Drain the potatoes and mash them until they're smooth.

- Preheat the oven to 180°C and line a square baking tin (23 x 23 cm) with greaseproof paper.

- In a large mixing bowl, add the mashed sweet potato, almond butter, cocoa powder, sugar, flour, baking powder and vanilla extract, and stir until well combined (it should look like a smooth batter).

- Fold in the chocolate chips and pour the mixture into your prepared baking tin.

- Bake for 40 minutes or until the edges start to come away from the sides of the tin.

- Let the brownies cool completely before cutting into 16 squares.

- Serve immediately, or store in an airtight container for up to three days.

I MAKE CHOCOLATE
DISAPPEAR – WHAT'S
YOUR SUPERPOWER?

· · · · · · · · · ·   · · · · · · ·

If there's no chocolate in
heaven, I'm not going.

JANE SEABROOK

· ·

Easy Chocolate Fudge

MAKES 20 SQUARES

INGREDIENTS

- 350 g dark chocolate chips
- 397 g can condensed milk
- 1 tsp vanilla extract

METHOD

- Line a square baking tin (23 x 23 cm) with greaseproof paper, making sure to cover the sides as well as the base.

- Place the chocolate chips and condensed milk into a large heatproof bowl and microwave on full power for 1 minute. Stir until all the chocolate chips have melted.

- Stir in the vanilla extract and transfer the mixture to the lined pan. Spread evenly.

- Let the fudge cool to room temperature before cutting into bite-sized squares.

- Store in an airtight container in the fridge for up to two weeks.

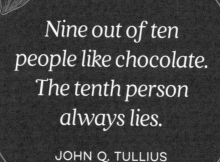

Nine out of ten people like chocolate. The tenth person always lies.

JOHN Q. TULLIUS

CHOCOLATEY FACT

One chocolate chip provides an
average adult with enough energy
to walk 46 metres (150 feet).

Chocolate Hazelnut Spread

MAKES 2 JARS

INGREDIENTS

- 200 g blanched hazelnuts
- 100 g milk chocolate
- 100 g dark chocolate
- 397 g tin condensed milk
- 4 tbsp vegetable oil
- 1 tbsp water

METHOD

- Sterilize your jars by washing them in hot soapy water, leaving them to dry on a roasting tray and then putting in to the oven at 170°C for 15 minutes.

- Preheat the oven to 180°C. Scatter the hazelnuts on a baking tray and toast for 5 minutes, until beginning to brown. Leave to cool before whizzing them in a food processor until finely ground.

- Break the chocolate into small pieces and place in a heatproof bowl over a pan of simmering water (make sure the bowl isn't touching the water), together with the condensed milk and the oil. Stir until melted and well combined.

- Pour the mixture into the food processor with the hazelnuts and add a tablespoon of water.

- Blend the mixture until it reaches the desired consistency, adding more water if needed.

- Spoon the spread into your sterilized jars while the mixture is still warm.

- Leave to cool while the lids are off then seal and store in the fridge for up to one month.

I love you a

CHOCO-LOT

. . . .

Giving chocolate to others is an intimate form of communication, a sharing of deep, dark secrets.

MILTON ZELMA

Chocolate Salted Caramel Cups

MAKES 12

INGREDIENTS

- 480 g milk chocolate
- 3 tbsp vegetable oil
- 200 g soft caramels
- 3 tbsp evaporated milk
- ¼ tsp salt

METHOD

- Line a cupcake tin with 12 cupcake cases and set aside.

- Break the chocolate into pieces and place it in a heatproof bowl over a pan of simmering water (make sure the bowl isn't touching the water), together with the oil. Stir until melted and well combined.

- Add 2 tablespoons of the chocolate mix into the cupcake cases and use a pastry brush to brush the chocolate up the sides of each case. Make sure to save enough to top them all with chocolate later.

- Put the tin in the fridge for the chocolate cases to harden while you make the filling.

- Add the caramels and evaporated milk into a heatproof bowl and repeat the same process as for the chocolate. Stir in the salt.

- Allow the mixture to cool in the fridge for 10 minutes.

- Divide the caramel evenly between the cupcake cases.

- Top the caramel with the remaining chocolate and freeze the cups until fully set (around 30 minutes).

- Serve immediately, or store in an airtight container in the fridge for up to five days.

CHOCOLATE IS GROUND FROM THE BEANS OF HAPPINESS.

TERRI GUILLEMETS

CHOCOLATEY FACT

Dark chocolate, consumed in moderation,
can help to reduce the risk of cardiovascular
disease; this is due to the flavonoids
in cocoa, which have been shown to
help lower blood pressure, improve
blood flow and fight cell damage.

Churros with Hot Chocolate Dip

MAKES 16 CHURROS

INGREDIENTS

For the churros:
- 250 ml water
- 6 tbsp unsalted butter
- 2 tbsp caster sugar
- 1 tsp vanilla extract
- 130 g plain flour
- ½ tsp salt
- 2 eggs

- Vegetable oil, for frying
- Cinnamon sugar, for coating

For the dipping sauce:
- 150 g dark chocolate chips
- 200 ml double cream
- ¼ tsp salt

METHOD

- In a large saucepan, add the water, butter and sugar and bring to the boil. Once the sugar has dissolved, turn off the heat and add in the vanilla extract, flour and salt. Stir until thickened, then set aside to cool for 15 minutes.

- Once the mixture is cooled, beat in the eggs until combined and transfer the mixture to a piping bag.

- Half fill a large pot with oil and heat (on the hob) to 190°C. Carefully pipe the churro mixture into the pan in 15 cm tubes (the batter may split if this is not done slowly).

- Deep fry the churros until golden (5 minutes), turning as necessary. Fry multiple churros (around three or four) at a time and let the oil come back to 190°C before each batch.

- Remove the churros with tongs and roll in cinnamon sugar while still piping hot. Place on a wire rack to cool.

- Place the chocolate and cream into a heatproof bowl and set on top of a pan of simmering water (make sure the bowl isn't touching the water). Stir the mixture occasionally until the chocolate has fully melted. Remove from the heat, then add the salt and whisk to combine.

- Serve immediately.

So many chocolates,

SO LITTLE TIME

· ·

There's nothing better
than a good friend,
except a good friend
with chocolate.

LINDA GRAYSON

Chocolate Banana Shake

VEGAN

MAKES 1 GLASS

INGREDIENTS
- 1 large ripe banana
- 2 pitted dates
- 2 tbsp peanut butter
- 1 tbsp cocoa powder
- ¼ tsp salt
- 300 ml non-dairy milk

METHOD
- Add the banana, dates, peanut butter, cocoa powder and salt into a food processor.

- Add in a small amount of milk before blending, then continue to add the milk a little at a time until the mixture reaches the desired consistency (use more milk for a thinner shake).

- Adjust flavours to taste and add a handful of ice to add thickness.

LOOK,
THERE'S NO
METAPHYSICS
ON EARTH LIKE
CHOCOLATES.

FERNANDO PESSOA

CHOCOLATEY FACT

Joseph Fry invented the first
chocolate bar in 1847.

Gluten-Free Chocolate Muffins

MAKES 12

INGREDIENTS

- 190 g gluten-free flour
- 125 g granulated sugar
- ½ tsp baking powder
- 1 tsp bicarboate of soda
- 50 g cocoa powder
- 75 g unsalted butter
- 2 large eggs
- 1 tsp vanilla extract
- 250 ml whole milk
- 100 g dark chocolate chips

METHOD

- Preheat the oven to 170°C and line a muffin tin with 12 muffin cases.

- Add the flour, sugar, baking powder, bicarboate of soda and cocoa powder into a mixing bowl and stir together to combine.

- Put the butter in a saucepan over a low heat and stir until melted.

- Pour the melted butter into a large heatproof bowl and add in the eggs, vanilla extract and milk.

- Mix the dry ingredients into the wet ingredients until they form a smooth batter. Then mix in the chocolate chips.

- Scoop the batter into the muffin cases, ensuring an even amount goes into each case.

- Bake the muffins for 20–25 minutes, or until a skewer comes out clean.

- Allow the muffins to cool completely before serving.

It's always

CHOCOLATE
TIME

· · · · · · ·

The 12-step chocoholics programme: never be more than 12 steps away from chocolate!

TERRY MOORE

Chocolate and Walnut Brownies

MAKES 9

INGREDIENTS

- 225 g unsalted butter, softened, plus a little extra for greasing
- 200 g caster sugar
- 2 large eggs
- 125 g plain flour
- 100 g unsweetened cocoa powder
- ½ tsp baking powder
- ¼ tsp salt
- 4 tbsp chopped walnuts

METHOD

- Preheat the oven to 180°C and grease and line a square baking tin (23 x 23 cm).

- Place the butter and sugar into a mixing bowl and beat the mixture until creamy.

- Beat in the eggs until the mixture forms a smooth batter, then sift in the flour, cocoa powder, baking powder and salt.

- Fold the dry ingredients into the wet mixture until just incorporated.

- Pour the mixture into the baking tin and scatter the walnuts over the top.

- Bake in a preheated oven until the brownies start to shrink away from the sides of the tin (25–30 minutes).

- Let the brownies cool completely in the tin, then cut into nine squares. Store in an airtight container in the fridge for up to three days.

WHEN IT COMES TO CHOCOLATE, RESISTANCE IS FUTILE.

REGINA BRETT

CHOCOLATEY FACT

In the Aztec civilization, it was documented that
a slave could be bought for 100 cocoa beans.

Dark Chocolate and Cherry Bars

MAKES 6

INGREDIENTS:

- 100 g amaretti biscuits, crushed
- 100 g dried cherries
- 400 g dark chocolate (minimum 60% cocoa solids)
- 400 ml double cream

METHOD

- Line a square baking tin (23 x 23 cm) with greaseproof paper, making sure some of the paper hangs over the side of the tray.

- Scatter the amaretti biscuits into the tin and mix with the dried cherries to form the base of the bar.

- Break the chocolate in to a heatproof bowl.

- Pour the cream into a saucepan and bring to the boil.

- Pour the cream over the chocolate pieces and leave for a minute to melt before stirring the mix into a chocolate sauce.

- Pour the chocolate mixture over the biscuits and make sure the surface is even.

- Cover the tin with cling film and chill in the fridge overnight.

- When set, use the baking paper to lift the bar out of the tin and use a sharp knife to cut into six bars.

- Serve immediately or store in an airtight container in the fridge for up to 3 days.

NOCHOCOPHOBIA
(NOUN.): THE FEAR
OF RUNNING OUT
OF CHOCOLATE

ONCE IN A
WHILE I SAY, "GO
FOR IT," AND I
EAT CHOCOLATE.

CLAUDIA SCHIFFER

Rocky Road

MAKES 18 BITES

INGREDIENTS

- 225 g dark chocolate (minimum 70% cocoa solids)
- 100 g unsalted butter
- 2 tbsp golden syrup
- 150 g milk chocolate digestives
- 100 g white chocolate chips
- 60 g mini marshmallows

METHOD

- Break the chocolate into pieces and place into a heatproof bowl with the butter and syrup. Heat the bowl over a pan of simmering water (make sure the bowl isn't touching the water) for 5–10 minutes, stirring all the time, until melted. Set the mixture aside.

- Break up the biscuits and fold into the chocolate mixture with the white chocolate chips and the mini marshmallows.

- Spoon the mixture into a square baking tin (23 x 23 cm).

- Place the tin in the fridge overnight to set.

- Use a sharp knife to cut nine squares

- Store in an airtight container for up to three days.

CHOCOLATEY FACT

In the 1960 Alfred Hitchcock film
Psycho, the "blood" in the famous shower
scene was actually chocolate syrup.

MY FAVOURITE THING IN THE WORLD IS A BOX OF FINE EUROPEAN CHOCOLATES WHICH IS, FOR SURE, BETTER THAN SEX.

ALICIA SILVERSTONE

Chocolate Tray Bake

MAKES 18 SLICES

INGREDIENTS

For the sponge:

- 50 g cocoa powder
- 6 tbsp boiling water
- 100 g unsalted butter
- 275 g caster sugar
- 120 ml whole milk
- 175 g self-raising flour
- 3 large eggs
- 1 tsp baking powder

For the icing:

- 200 g dark chocolate
- 300 ml double cream
- 2 tbsp golden caster sugar

METHOD

- Preheat the oven to 180°C and line a square baking tin (23 x 23 cm) with baking paper.

- Sift the cocoa powder into a large bowl, add the boiling water then mix until smooth.

- Add the butter and beat with the cocoa until combined.

- Add the rest of the sponge ingredients and mix until it forms a batter.

- Pour the cake mixture into the tin and bake in the preheated oven for 35–40 minutes, until the cake has risen and a skewer comes out clean.

- Leave for 15 minutes to cool slightly, then turn out of the tin onto a wire rack and leave to cool completely.

- While the cake cools, make the icing by breaking the chocolate into pieces and putting it into a large heatproof mixing bowl. Pour the cream into a saucepan with the sugar and bring to a simmer, stirring continuously until the sugar has dissolved.

- Bring the cream and sugar mixture to the boil and immediately pour over the broken chocolate. Whisk until smooth.

- When the cake is cool, use a palette knife to spread the icing over the cake and cover it completely. Cut the cake into 18 slices and serve.

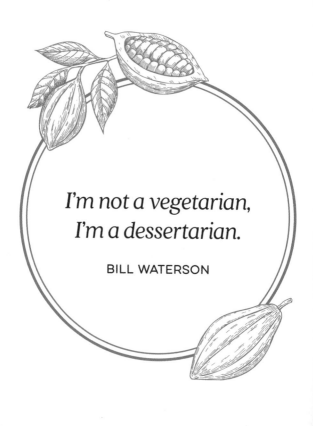

I'm not a vegetarian,
I'm a dessertarian.

BILL WATERSON

Life happens,

CHOCOLATE
HELPS

· · · · · · · · · ·

Chocolate Fondant

MAKES 4

INGREDIENTS

- 50 g unsalted butter, plus extra for greasing
- 2 tsp cocoa powder, to dust
- 50 g dark chocolate (minimum 70% cocoa solids)
- 1 large egg
- 1 egg yolk
- 60 g caster sugar
- 50 g plain flour

METHOD

- Preheat the oven to 160°C. Grease four ramekins, then dust with cocoa powder.

- Break the chocolate into small pieces and place in a heatproof bowl over a pan of simmering water (make sure the bowl isn't touching the water), together with the butter. Stir until melted and well combined.

- In a separate mixing bowl, beat the egg, egg yolk and sugar until pale and creamy, then fold in the chocolate mixture, followed by the flour.

- Divide the mixture between the ramekins and bake in the oven for 10–12 minutes.

- Turn the fondants out onto a warm plate and serve.

CHOCOLATEY FACT

According to some research, eating chocolate releases more endorphins in the brain than kissing.

· · · · · · · · · ·   · · · · · · ·

After eating chocolate,
you feel godlike, as though
you can conquer enemies,
lead armies, entice lovers.

EMILY LUCHETTI

· ·

Chocolate Oat Biscuits

VEGAN

MAKES 25

INGREDIENTS

- 100 g rolled oats
- 125 g plain flour
- 150 g golden caster sugar
- 100 ml vegetable oil
- 2 tbsp golden syrup
- 1 tsp baking powder
- 3 tbsp hot water
- 150 g dark chocolate (minimum 70% cocoa solids)

METHOD

- Preheat the oven to 160°C and line two baking trays with greaseproof paper.

- Mix the oats, flour and sugar in a mixing bowl.

- Pour the oil and syrup into a saucepan and melt them together over a medium heat. Remove from the heat and pour into another mixing bowl.

- Mix the baking powder with hot water in a small dish, then add to the oil and syrup mixture.

- Pour the wet ingredients over the dry ingredients and mix well to form a dough.

- Roll the dough into balls and space them evenly on the trays (ensure at least 5 cm distance between each ball). Flatten the balls with your palm.

- Bake for 12–15 minutes until golden brown. Remove from the oven and leave to firm up for 10 minutes.

- Transfer the biscuits to a wire rack to cool completely.

- Break the chocolate into a heatproof bowl on top of a pan of simmering water (make sure the bowl isn't touching the water), stirring occasionally until melted.

- Once the biscuits are cooled, spoon melted dark chocolate over the biscuits and use a palette knife to flatten.

- Store in an airtight container at room temperature for up to three days.

Don't wreck a sublime chocolate experience by feeling guilty.

LORA BRODY

WHEN LIFE GIVES
YOU LEMONS... THROW
THEM BACK AND ASK
FOR CHOCOLATE

Chocolate and Peanut Butter "Nice Cream"

VEGAN

SERVES 4

INGREDIENTS

- 4 frozen overripe bananas
- 65 g peanut butter
- 35 g cocoa powder
- ½ tsp vanilla extract
- ¼ tsp salt

- Splash non-dairy milk, optional
- Peanuts, for serving, optional

METHOD

- Combine all the ingredients in a food processor.

- Blend until completely smooth, adding a little non-dairy milk to loosen the mixture if needed.

- Serve immediately, topping with crushed peanuts (if desired).

CHOCOLATEY FACT

The global consumption of chocolate every year
is estimated to be at least 7.2 million tonnes.

I WANT TO HAVE A
GOOD BODY, BUT
NOT AS MUCH AS I
WANT DESSERT.

JASON LOVE

Chocolate Bean Dip

VEGAN

SERVES 4

INGREDIENTS

- 30 g dark chocolate (minimum 85% cocoa solids)
- 3 tbsp olive oil
- 1 large onion
- 300 ml vegetable stock
- 1 tbsp tomato paste
- 1 tsp chilli powder
- 1 tsp cumin
- 1 tsp paprika
- 1 tsp coriander
- 2 tsp salt
- 400 g tin black beans, drained and rinsed
- 1 tsp agave syrup
- 200 g tinned tomatoes

METHOD

- Break the chocolate into a bowl and set aside.

- Put a large saucepan on a medium heat and add the oil.

- Dice the onion and add it to the pan, frying until it is translucent.

- Pour in the vegetable stock and bring to a simmer.

- Add the tomato paste, spices and salt and stir well.

- Add in the black beans, dark chocolate, agave syrup and tomatoes.

- Allow the sauce to cook for around 10 minutes, or until the liquid has reduced down.

- Keep the sauce simmering until the desired consistency is reached (longer if you like a thicker dip).

- Serve with tortilla chips or taquitos as a dipping sauce.

- Leftovers are great when thinned down with water and enjoyed as a soup.

CHOCOLATE
IS MEDICINAL.
I JUST DID
ANOTHER
STUDY THAT
CONFIRMS IT.

MICHELLE M. PILLOW

THE ONLY THING BETTER
THAN CHOCOLATE IS
MORE CHOCOLATE

Chocolate Shortbread

MAKES 10

INGREDIENTS

- 175 g unsalted butter
- 85 g golden caster sugar
- 200 g plain flour
- 150 g milk chocolate chips

METHOD

- Put the butter and sugar into a large mixing bowl and beat until creamy.

- Sift in the flour and fold until well combined.

- Add in the chocolate chips and mix together with your hands, to ensure even dispersal of the chocolate.

- Halve the dough and roll each half into a cylinder (with a 6 cm diameter).

- Wrap the dough in cling film and chill in the fridge for 1–2 hours.

- Heat the oven to 180°C. Remove the cling film and slice the logs into 1 cm thick rounds and place on a lined baking tray.

- Bake the shortbread in the oven for 10–12 minutes, or until they are golden brown.

- Let the biscuits rest on the tray for 10 minutes, then transfer to a wire rack to cool completely.

- Store in an airtight container at room temperature for up to three days.

CHOCOLATEY FACT

In 1981, M&Ms were the first
chocolates to go to outer space.

*And above all,
think chocolate!*

BETTY CROCKER

Chocolate Orange Cupcakes

MAKES 12

INGREDIENTS

For the cupcakes:

- 125 g unsalted butter
- 125 g caster sugar
- 2 eggs
- 100 g dark orange chocolate
- 125 g self-raising flour
- 1 tbsp milk

For the buttercream:

- 200 g unsalted butter
- 400 g icing sugar
- 1 tbsp water

METHOD

- Preheat the oven to 180°C and line a cupcake tin with 12 cupcake cases.

- Beat the butter and sugar together until creamy, then add the eggs and beat well again.

- Break the chocolate into pieces and place in a heatproof bowl over a pan of simmering water (make sure the bowl isn't touching the water) until melted, then stir it into the butter mixture.

- Sift the flour and fold it into the mixture until smooth. Stir in the milk to loosen the mixture slightly.

- Spoon the cake mixture into the cupcake cases and divide evenly between them.

- Bake the cupcakes for 25 minutes (or until a skewer comes out clean) and leave to cool.

- Meanwhile, to make the buttercream, use an electric whisk to beat the butter until it's smooth. Add a teaspoon of water and then whisk in the icing sugar, a little at a time, until the mixture is spreadable.

- Put the buttercream in a piping bag and, once the cakes are cool, pipe a swirl on top of each.

- Store in an airtight container at room temperature for up to three days.

What you see
before you, my
friend, is the result
of a lifetime
of chocolate.

KATHARINE HEPBURN

The magic ingredient is always

CHOCOLATE

· · · · · · · · · · · · · · · · · · · ·

Cinnamon Hot Chocolate

VEGAN OPTION

MAKES 2 MUGS

INGREDIENTS

- 500 ml milk (or non-dairy alternative)
- 2 tbsp granulated sugar
- 175 g dark chocolate, plus a little extra for decoration
- ½ tsp ground cinnamon
- 2 cinnamon sticks (optional)

METHOD

- In a large saucepan, over a medium heat, combine the milk and sugar, and bring to a simmer (ensuring that it doesn't boil, as this could burn the mixture).

- Break the chocolate into pieces and place it in a heatproof bowl over a pan of simmering water (make sure the bowl isn't touching the water) until melted.

- Pour the chocolate into the milk and sugar mixture, add in the cinnamon and whisk to combine.

- Pour into two mugs and serve with a cinnamon stick and grated chocolate (if desired).

CHOCOLATEY FACT

Cocoa trees can live for up to 200 years, but only produce good-quality cocoa beans for around 25 years.

ONE CANNOT
THINK WELL,
LOVE WELL,
SLEEP WELL, IF
ONE HAS NOT
DINED WELL.

VIRGINIA WOOLF

S'mores Dip

SERVES 6

INGREDIENTS

- 100 g milk chocolate
- 100 g dark chocolate
- 100 ml double cream
- 100 ml condensed milk
- 150 g marshmallows
- 50 g mini marshmallows
- Dippables, such as digestives, cake pops or shortbread

METHOD

- Preheat your grill to a high heat.

- Break up both types of chocolate into a heatproof bowl and add in the cream and the condensed milk. Place the bowl over a pan of simmering water, making sure it doesn't touch the water.

- Allow the chocolate to melt into the cream and the condensed milk, then stir until the mixture is smooth.

- Transfer the chocolate sauce to an ovenproof dish, to create the bottom layer of the dip.

- Arrange the larger marshmallows over the chocolate layer, then scatter over the mini marshmallows so that the chocolate is no longer visible.

- Place the bowl under the grill and cook for 4–5 minutes or until the marshmallows are toasted on the surface.

- Serve immediately with your choice of dippables.

CHOCOLATE IS A
PERFECT FOOD, AS
WHOLESOME AS IT
IS DELICIOUS.

JUSTUS VON LIEBIG

DID YOU EVER NOTICE
THERE ARE NO RECIPES
FOR LEFTOVER
CHOCOLATE?

Raw Chocolate Brownies

VEGAN

MAKES 10

INGREDIENTS

For the brownies:
- 100 g medjool dates, pitted
- 50 g dried goji berries
- 100 g almond butter
- 50 g chopped pistachios
- 50 g coconut oil
- 2 tbsp agave syrup
- 50 g dark chocolate (minimum 70% cocoa solids)
- 50 g cocoa powder

For the drizzle:
- 75 g dark chocolate

METHOD

- Put all the ingredients for the brownies into a blender and blitz until well combined.

- Spoon the mixture into a square baking tin (23 x 23 cm) and flatten the surface.

- Put the tin into the freezer for 20 minutes to firm up the brownie mix.

- Meanwhile, for the drizzle, break the chocolate into pieces and place it in a heatproof bowl over a pan of simmering water (make sure the bowl isn't touching the water) until melted.

- Drizzle the melted chocolate over the brownies using a spoon.

- Cut into ten squares and store in an airtight container for up to three days.

CHOCOLATEY FACT

In 2017, the Belgian-Swiss cocoa company, Barry Callebaut, introduced a product they marketed as the fourth variety of chocolate (after dark, milk and white): ruby chocolate. The chocolate is said to have a sweet yet sour flavour, but its production methods have remained a trade secret.

Sometimes a girl's gotta have some chocolate!

CARRIE UNDERWOOD

Chocolate Bread and Butter Pudding

SERVES 6

INGREDIENTS

- 40 g unsalted butter, plus extra for greasing
- 8 slices white bread
- 50 g dried cranberries
- 100 g dark chocolate (minimum 70% cocoa solids)
- 400 ml whole milk
- 50 ml double cream
- 70 g caster sugar
- 3 eggs

METHOD

- Preheat the oven to 180°C and grease a square baking tin (23 x 23 cm).

- Cut the crusts off the bread, lightly butter each slice, then cut the slices in half to form triangles.

- Arrange half the slices (buttered side up) at the bottom of the tray and scatter over half the dried cranberries. Then add the remaining bread and scatter the rest of the cranberries.

- Break the chocolate into pieces and place it in a heatproof bowl over a pan of simmering water (make sure the bowl isn't touching the water), together with the milk, cream and sugar. Heat and stir until the chocolate has melted and the sugar has dissolved.

- Whisk the eggs in a bowl, then gradually add the milk mixture, whisking continuously.

- Pour the mixture over the bread and leave the dish for 20 minutes so it can be absorbed as much as possible.

- Place the dish in the oven and bake for 25–30 minutes, until browning on the surface.

- Leave to cool a little before serving.

- Store in an airtight container in the fridge for up to three days.

RESEARCH TELLS US FOURTEEN OUT OF ANY TEN INDIVIDUALS LIKE CHOCOLATE.

SANDRA BOYNTON

SNACCIDENT (NOUN.):
EATING A FAMILY-SIZED
BAR OF CHOCOLATE
ENTIRELY BY MISTAKE

Chocolate Chilli Barbeque Sauce

VEGAN

MAKES 5 CUPS

INGREDIENTS

- 2 tbsp olive oil
- 2 onions, finely chopped
- 5 garlic cloves, minced
- 3 tbsp chilli powder
- 35 g cocoa powder
- 2 140 g tins tomato puree
- 330 ml dark beer
- 220 ml apple cider vinegar
- 220 ml molasses
- 120 ml balsamic vinegar
- 3 tbsp soy sauce

METHOD

- Heat the oil in a large saucepan and add in the onions. Sautee gently for 5 minutes, or until translucent.

- Add in the garlic and cook for 1 minute, then add the chilli and cocoa powder.

- Cook until fragrant, then add the remaining ingredients and cook for 40–45 minutes over a medium heat.

- Remove the saucepan from the heat and allow the sauce to cool until no longer steaming.

- Pour the sauce into a blender and puree until smooth.

- Decant the sauce into an airtight container and store in the fridge for up to one week.

CHOCOLATEY FACT

In 2018, nine chocolate bars were discovered in a tin that belonged to a World War One British soldier. The 103-year-old chocolate was sold in an auction, together with cigarettes, medals and letters, for over £3,000.

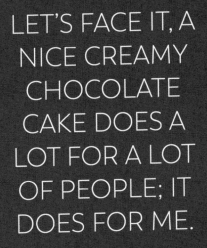

LET'S FACE IT, A NICE CREAMY CHOCOLATE CAKE DOES A LOT FOR A LOT OF PEOPLE; IT DOES FOR ME.

AUDREY HEPBURN

Strawberry Salad with Chocolate Vinaigrette

VEGAN

SERVES 2

INGREDIENTS

For the salad:

- 4 tbsp walnuts
- 600 g rocket leaves
- 200 g spinach leaves
- 1 green apple, cored and thinly sliced
- 150 g strawberries, hulled and sliced

For the vinaigrette:

- 6 tbsp dark chocolate chips
- 6 tbsp balsamic vinegar
- 6 tbsp olive oil
- 3 tsp agave syrup
- 1 tsp salt
- ½ tsp black pepper

METHOD

- Preheat the oven to 180°C. Arrange the walnuts on a baking tray (lined with baking paper) and bake them in the oven for 8–10 minutes, checking frequently.

- To make the vinaigrette, put the chocolate chips in a heatproof bowl over a pan of simmering water (make sure the bowl isn't touching the water) until melted.

- Remove the chocolate from the heat, and stir in the balsamic vinegar, oil, agave syrup, salt and pepper, then leave to cool in the fridge.

- While the vinaigrette cools, divide the rocket and spinach leaves between two plates, and top with apple and strawberry slices.

- Drizzle with the vinaigrette and top with the toasted walnuts.

- Serve immediately.

Chocolate is cheaper than
therapy and you don't
need an appointment.

ANONYMOUS

Chocolate:

THE OTHER
VITAMIN C

· · · · · · · · · · · · · · · ·

Chocolate Pancakes

MAKES 16

INGREDIENTS

For the pancakes:
- 225 g self-raising flour
- 50 g cocoa powder
- 1 tsp baking powder
- 1 tbsp caster sugar
- 2 eggs
- 400 ml whole milk
- 1 tbsp vegetable oil
- 50 g unsalted butter

For the topping:
- 300 ml chocolate syrup
- Small bar dark chocolate, broken into pieces
- Handful walnuts, chopped

METHOD

- Put the flour, cocoa powder, baking powder and sugar into a bowl, then add the eggs and milk, and whisk until you form a batter.

- Heat the oil and the butter in a frying pan and cook the pancakes for one minute on each side, using a ladleful of batter for each pancake. Flip the pancakes halfway through.

- To serve, stack the pancakes and pour over your syrup. Sprinkle chocolate and walnuts over the top.

CHOCOLATEY FACT

The smell of chocolate increases theta
brain waves, which can induce relaxation.

ANY MONTH
WHOSE NAME
CONTAINS THE
LETTER A, E, OR
U IS THE PROPER
TIME FOR
CHOCOLATE.

SANDRA BOYNTON

Chocolate Chilli con Carne

VEGAN OPTION
SERVES 4

INGREDIENTS

- 1 tbsp olive oil
- 1 onion, finely chopped
- 2 red peppers, chopped
- 1 tsp hot chilli powder
- 2 tsp paprika
- 1 tsp cumin
- 500 g beef mince (or plant-based mince alternative)

- 500 ml passata
- 250 ml beef or vegetable stock
- 25 g dark chocolate (minimum 70% cocoa solids)
- 400 g can kidney beans
- 230 g of uncooked white rice

METHOD

- Heat the oil in a large saucepan over a medium heat.

- Add in the onion and sautee gently for 3 minutes until it starts to look translucent.

- Add in the peppers and cook for a further 3 minutes.

- Add the spices to the pan and stir for one minute until it is fragrant.

- Add the mince to the pan and cook according to pack instructions. If using beef mince, make sure it is browned all over before moving on to the next step.

- Pour in the passata and stock.

- Bring to mixture to the boil and then let it simmer for 30 minutes.

- Chop the chocolate and add it into the chilli, along with the kidney beans.

- Stir well and then simmer for a further 10 minutes, until the mixture has started to thicken.

- While the chilli is simmering, boil the rice until fully cooked (according to pack instructions).

- Serve immediately.

- Store any leftovers in an airtight container for up to 3 days in the fridge, or in the freezer for up to 4 months.

YOU CAN'T MAKE
EVERYONE HAPPY –
YOU'RE NOT CHOCOLATE

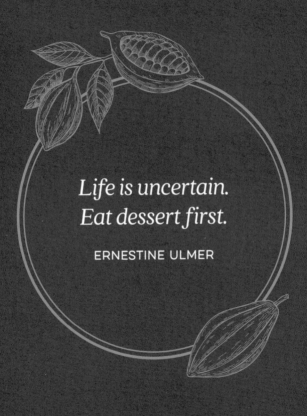

Life is uncertain.
Eat dessert first.

ERNESTINE ULMER

White Chocolate and Hazelnut Fudge

MAKES 20 SQUARES

INGREDIENTS
- 397 g tin condensed milk
- 100 g unsalted butter
- 280 g caster sugar
- 1 tbsp golden syrup
- 150 g white chocolate chips
- 65 g roasted hazelnuts

METHOD
- Line a square baking tin (23 x 23 cm) with greaseproof paper.

- In a saucepan, combine the condensed milk, butter, sugar and golden syrup.

- Bring the mixture to the boil, stirring continuously.

- Boil for 10 minutes, then remove from the heat.

- Stir in the chocolate until it is melted and the mixture is smooth, then mix in the roasted hazelnuts.

- Pour into the prepared tin and spread evenly.

- Allow to cool completely before cutting into squares.

CHOCOLATEY FACT

Chocolate contains a number of mood-boosting chemicals, including phenylethylamine (a natural anti-depressant) and tryptophan (a chemical linked to the production of serotonin).

Carpe cocoa:

SEIZE THE
CHOCOLATE!

· · · · · · · · · · · · · · · · · · ·

Chocolate Empanadas

MAKES 10

INGREDIENTS

For the dough:
- 275 g plain flour, plus extra for dusting
- 1 tsp baking powder
- 1 tsp salt
- 60 g unsalted butter
- 80 ml cold water

For the filling and garnish:
- 100 g milk chocolate
- Icing sugar, for dusting

METHOD

- To make the dough, sift the flour, baking powder and salt into a large mixing bowl and combine.

- Melt the butter in a saucepan over a medium heat, then pour over the dry ingredients and stir well.

- Pour in the water, bit by bit, and incorporate into the mix until it forms a dough.

- Lightly flour a kitchen surface and knead the dough a few times. Shape the dough into a ball and wrap in cling film. Chill for 30 minutes.

- Once chilled, roll the dough out on a floured surface to a 0.5 cm thickness.

- Use a cookie cutter to cut out ten circles of 8–10 cm dough.

- Break the chocolate and place a little on each round of pastry (leaving a small border), and then fold the pastry over the chocolate to form semi-circles. Seal the edges well and crimp with a fork.

- Transfer the empanadas to a lined baking tray and place in the oven at 180°C. Bake for 25 minutes, or until golden brown.

- Remove from the oven and allow to cool a little before dusting with icing sugar.

- Serve immediately.

Index

Have you enjoyed this book? If so, find us on
Facebook at **Summersdale Publishers**, on
Twitter at **@Summersdale** and on Instagram at
@summersdalebooks and get in touch.
We'd love to hear from you!

www.summersdale.com